D1314268

I Am
Responsible

Mary Elizabeth Salzmann

Consulting Editor, Monica Marx, M.A./Reading Specialist

ABDO
Publishing Company

Published by SandCastle™, an imprint of ABDO Publishing Company, 4940 Viking Drive, Edina, Minnesota 55435.

Printed in the United States.

Credits
Edited by: Pam Price
Curriculum Coordinator: Nancy Tuminelly
Cover and Interior Design and Production: Mighty Media
Photo Credits: Digital Vision, Eyewire Images, PhotoDisc, Stockbyte

Library of Congress Cataloging-in-Publication Data

Salzmann, Mary Elizabeth, 1968-
    I am responsible / Mary Elizabeth Salzmann.
        p. cm. -- (Building character)
    Includes index.
    Summary: Defines responsibility as doing what you are supposed to do and provides some examples, such as taking care of yourself, taking care of other people, and following the rules.
    ISBN 1-57765-830-2
    1. Responsibility--Juvenile literature. 2. Children--Conduct of life--Juvenile literature.
[1. Responsibility. 2. Conduct of life.] I. Title.

BJ1451 .S25 2002
179'.9--dc21

                                                                        2002066407

SandCastle™ books are created by a professional team of educators, reading specialists, and content developers around five essential components that include phonemic awareness, phonics, vocabulary, text comprehension, and fluency. All books are written, reviewed, and leveled for guided reading, early intervention reading, and Accelerated Reader® programs and designed for use in shared, guided, and independent reading and writing activities to support a balanced approach to literacy instruction.

Let Us Know

After reading the book, SandCastle would like you to tell us your stories about reading. What is your favorite page? Was there something hard that you needed help with? Share the ups and downs of learning to read. We want to hear from you! To get posted on the ABDO Publishing Company Web site, send us email at:

sandcastle@abdopub.com

SandCastle Level: Transitional

Your character is the kind of person you are.

You show your character in the things you say and do.

Responsibility is part of your character.

3

I try to be responsible.

There are many ways to be responsible.

Being responsible means doing what you are supposed to do.

I practice the violin every day.

When I do my homework on time, I am being responsible.

Being responsible means taking care of yourself.

We brush our teeth every day.

I always wear my helmet when I ride my bike.

I am being responsible.

Being responsible means
taking care of other people.

I read to my little sister.

Being responsible means taking care of animals.

We feed the class hamster.

Being responsible means
following the rules.

I go to sleep when it is my
bedtime.

What do you do to be responsible?

Index

Glossary

bedtime the time you usually go to bed

hamster a small animal that many people keep as a pet

helmet a special hat you wear to protect your head

homework school assignments that you do at home

sister a girl who has the same mother or father as someone else

teeth the hard white parts of your mouth that you use to bite and chew

violin an instrument that makes music when you rub a bow across its strings

About SandCastle™

A professional team of educators, reading specialists, and content developers created the SandCastle™ series to support young readers as they develop reading skills and strategies and increase their general knowledge. The SandCastle™ series has four levels that correspond to early literacy development in young children. The levels are provided to help teachers and parents select the appropriate books for young readers.

Emerging Readers
(no flags)

Beginning Readers
(1 flag)

Transitional Readers
(2 flags)

Fluent Readers
(3 flags)

These levels are meant only as a guide. All levels are subject to change.

To see a complete list of SandCastle™ books and other nonfiction titles from ABDO Publishing Company, visit www.abdopub.com or contact us at:

4940 Viking Drive, Edina, Minnesota 55435 • 1-800-800-1312 • fax: 1-952-831-1632